BIKERS
ILLUSTRATED

BIKERS ILLUSTRATED

An American Lifestyle Coloring Book

By

JOHN "TEACH" GIRARD

ARPress
ILLUMINATING IDEAS.
EMPOWERING VOICES

ARPress
45 Dan Road Suite 5
Canton MA 02021

Hotline: 1(800) 220-7660
Fax: 1(855) 752-6001

Ordering Information:
Quantity sales. Special discounts are available on quantity purchases by corporations, associations, and others. For details, contact the publisher at the address above.

Printed in the United States of America.

ISBN-13:   Paperback   979-8-89389-873-6
              eBook   979-8-89389-874-3

Library of Congress Control Number: 2024923864

TEACH GIRARD
2013

1

ZACH GIRARD
2018

3

4

6

PEACE GERARD
2018

7

TEACH GIRARD
2008

8

11

Trace Girard
2018

12

13

14

15

16

17

TRACY GIRARD
2018

18

19

Teach Girard
2018

20

21

23

24

25

26

Teach Girard
2018

27

TEACH GIRARD
2018

28

Teach Girard
2018

30

31

Teach Gerard
2018

32

33

Teach Girard
2018

34

Teach Girard
2018

35

36

37

39

40

TEACH GODARD
2018

41

42

43

44

45

REACH GIRARD
2018

46

47

48

Teach Girard
2013

49

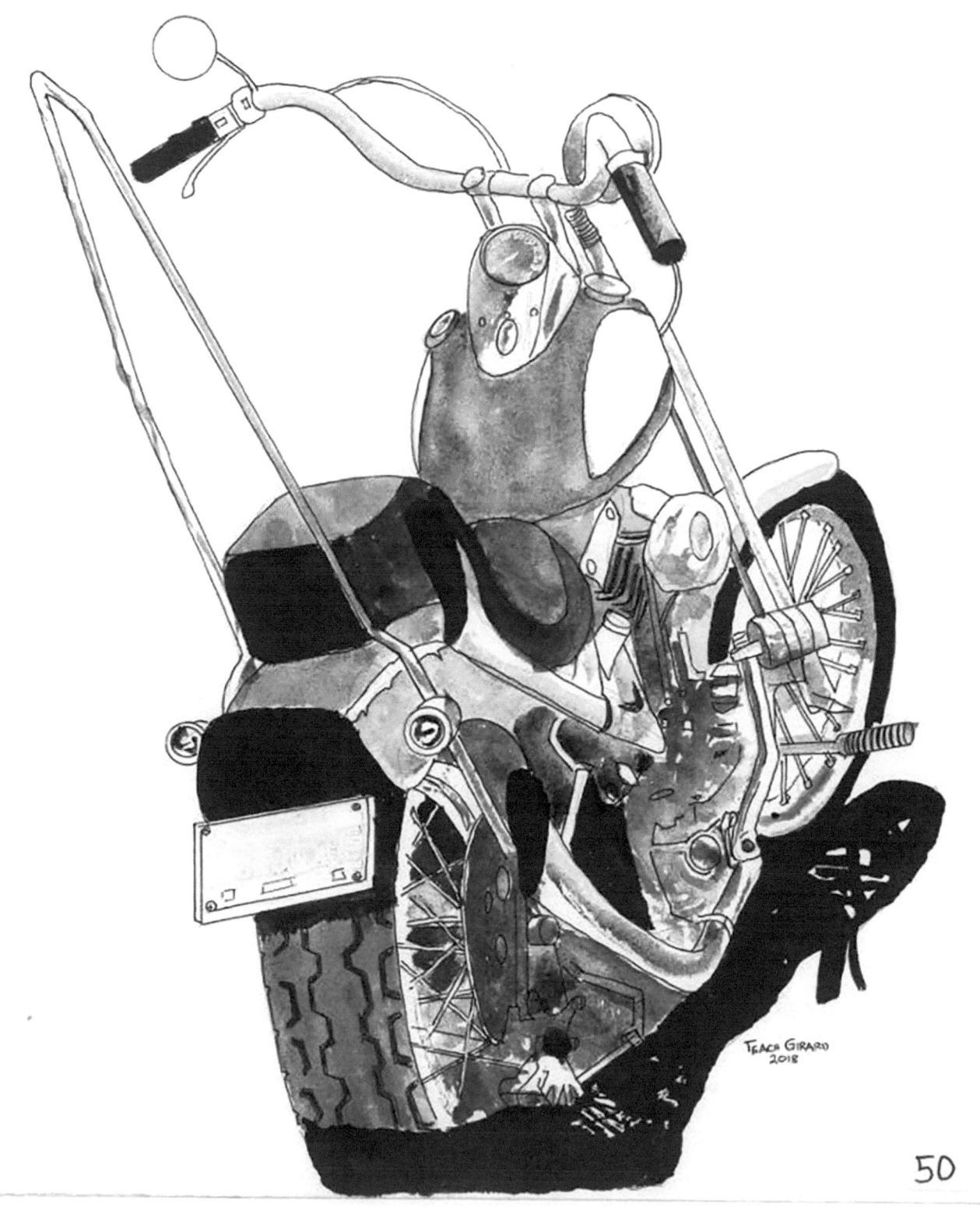

50

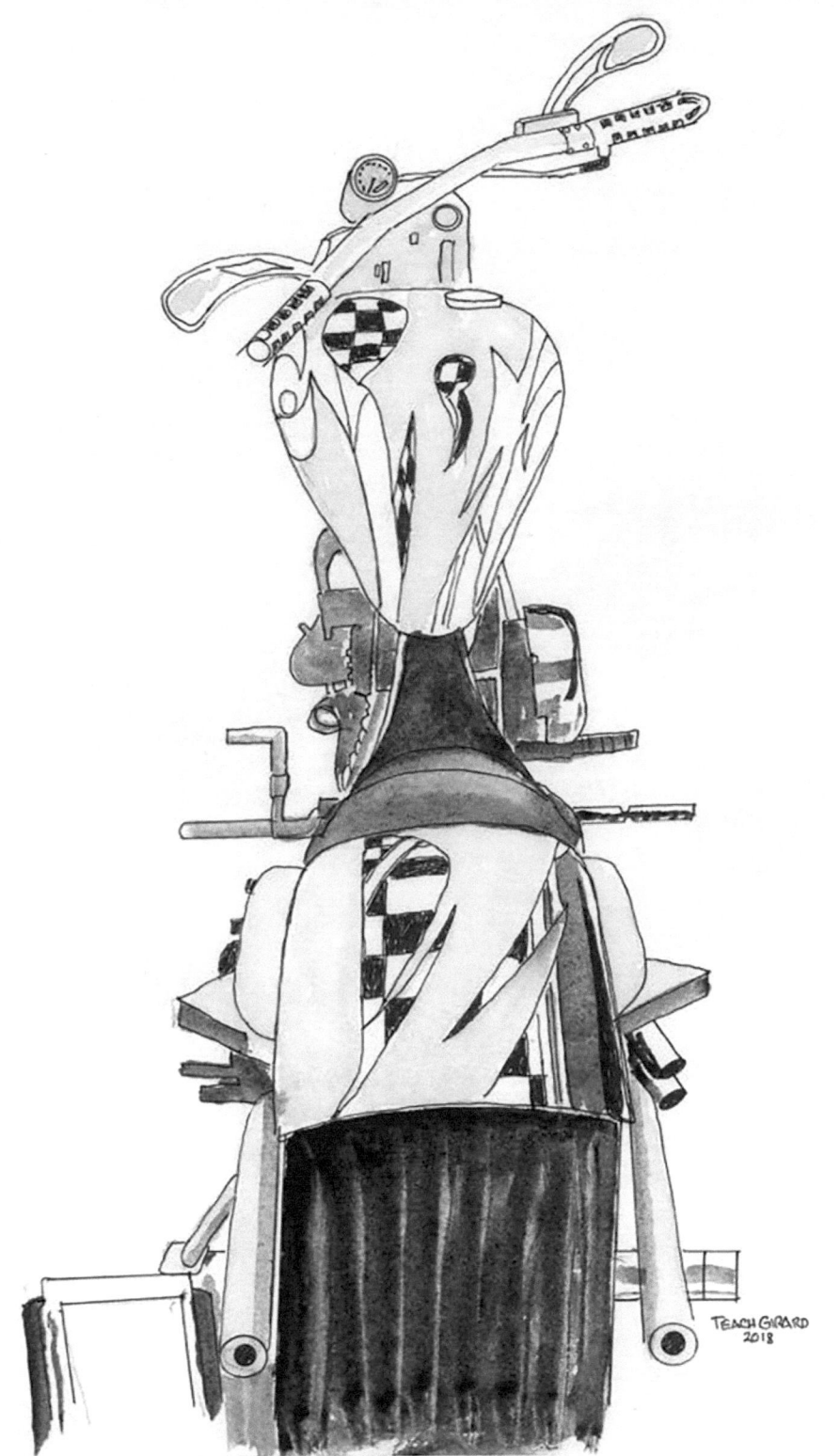

51

52

53

54

Teach Girard
2018

55

Jean Girard
2018

56

ABOUT THE AUTHOR

Born and raised in a small town in California, after high school, John "Teach" Girard joined the United States Air Force in 1964. While serving in the USAF, Girard acquired a blood-clotting disease called thrombophlebitis in which the blood clotted and the veins in his ankle were collapsing, resulting in no circulation to the feet. In 1976, both feet were amputated below his knees. After a medical retirement from the USAF, he went on to college at California State University, Sacramento and University of Oregon to complete his teaching certificate. With the help of his friends, he created unique knee controls on his Harley Davidson with a sidecar so he could continue his love for motorcycle riding. "Teach" taught arts and crafts in several school districts in Oregon. Now he is living in the Eugene, Oregon area with his family where he continues to illustrate transportation-related subjects, such as hot rods, trucks and motorcycles. His motto, "*defeeted but not defeated*" is tattooed on his arm. He continues to walk on his knees with the help of prosthetic knee pads and smile and a handshake for folks who see him and thank him for his military service.